THE
BOURNVILLE
HALLMARK

Housing People for 100 Years

BOURNVILLE VILLAGE

SUGGESTED RULES OF HEALTH

If you will follow the rules below you will be healthier and therefore more cheerful. You will probably live ten years longer than those who ignore them.

Do not take more than three meals a day. Have regular times and keep to them; allowing at least five hours between.

Take no solid food of any kind between meals; this rule applies with double force to children.

Do not take flesh meat more than once a day. The German army before Metz suffered much from disease; they were compelled to have largely a meat diet; when besieging Paris the amount of meat consumed was comparatively small and there was a remarkable absence of disease. All vegetables are most wholesome and of better flavour when cooked as soon as taken out of the garden; bake and stew as far as possible, the most valuable salts and properties are lost in the water when boiled. Use oatmeal porridge for breakfast.

Avoid intoxicating liquors, tobacco, pork, aerated drinks, and all drugs as far as possible.

Never allow water to stand on tea more than three minutes, or tannic acid is developed which is injurious.

Be sure that bread and other food is well cooked. Bakers' bread is improved by a second cooking, say 10 minutes in a hot oven.

Apples are the most wholesome fruit; they should be used freely, both raw and cooked.

When you come in tired, rest a few minutes before taking a meal.

Eat slowly, and always get up from the meal with an appetite.

SANITARY ARRANGEMENTS ETC

Furnish your sleeping apartments with single beds; double beds are now little used in civilised countries except in the United Kingdom. A mattress is much more healthy than a feather bed.

Take a cold bath, a sponge bath, or if you have neither, dip a towel in water and rub the body over with it, followed with a dry towel. Baths are provided in the back kitchens, so that it may be possible to have a warm bath at least once a week, without the expense of costly hot water apparatus and you have the advantage of drying by the fire.

Live in the open sunny air as much as possible.

Breathe through the nostrils with the mouth closed, especially at night.

Take walking or other exercise in the open air for at least half an hour daily.

Unless the weather is very damp and misty have your windows open at night and day. Every room is furnished with a Tobin ventilator, which should always be kept open, you thus have fresh air when fear of rain or snow would prevent opening the window.

Sleep is much more refreshing when the room is dark, so keep no artificial lights burning in it. Gas should never burn in a room without a door or window open as the fumes are very poisonous. One ordinary gas jet is calculated to consume as much oxygen as 12 to 14 persons besides giving off carbonic acid and other poisons.

If possible cultivate your garden with the help of your own family. Man's natural place is on the land. Work in a garden enlarges the minds and strengthens the bodies of your children.

Rest a least 8 hours of the 24, and if you cannot sleep all the time do not worry about it. If you lie flat upon your back the heart and all the organs of the body rest.

Rise early, and if possible get into the fresh morning air.

CLOTHING

Do not sleep in any clothing worn during the day. Do not wear tight waistbands, corsets, or anything that will interfere with the circulation.

The best clothing gives the largest amount of heat with the least possible weight.

Have boots made to fit the feet with wide soles and with low heels. Boots last much longer if the same pair is not worn two days in succession. In wet weather put them to dry gradually overnight at least 3 feet from the fire with soles towards it. Wear strong boots and keep your feet dry. Many a cold will be avoided by looking well to your boots and seeing that they are water tight. Always change them at once when coming into the house. Blacking destroys the leather; it is much more sensible to use dubbing all through the winter months.

Anger and worry will wear you out much more rapidly than hard work. Cultivate a cheerful and thankful spirit.

In a truly happy home Father and Mother will conduct family worship at least once a day when the Bible should be read and a hymn sung.

To each of the first residents on his estate George Cadbury issued this list of suggested Rules of Health

THE BOURNVILLE HALLMARK

Housing People for 100 Years

by

JUDY HILLMAN

BREWIN BOOKS

First Published in 1994 by Brewin Books,
Doric House, Church Street, Studley, Warks B80 7LG

ISBN 1 85858 053 6
© The Bournville Village Trust 1994

Acknowledgements

I would like to thank the Chairman, Chief Executive and other members of the
staff of the Bournville Trust, together with residents of the Bournville Estate,
William Muirhead and staff at the City Archives, Birmingham Central Library,
for so much generous help in researching this publication.

J.H.

British Library Cataloguing in Publication Data
A Catalogue record for this book is available from the British Library

Photography by Max Jones Tel: 0749 870440

Printed and bound in Great Britain by Warwick Printing Co Ltd
Theatre Street, Warwick CV34 4DR

Contents

Professor Gordon Cherry

Preface

The building of a number of houses in Mary Vale Road in 1895 signalled the beginning of the Bournville Estate. A few years later the laying out of roads in the vicinity of the factory marked the heart of an embryo garden village. No master plan guided this or subsequent development, but long-standing adherence to a set of design principles ensured a residential environment of charm and distinction.

Development has continued in various phases to the present day, each building unit with its own character. Today Bournville is known far and wide for its place in housing and town planning history.

In these circumstances it is appropriate, one hundred years on, to mark the centenary of the Estate with an account of the various elements of the housing story. There have been a number of histories of Bournville, but a new one was required, updated and written to appeal to the widest readership.

Judy Hillman was commissioned to undertake this task. Writer and environmental analyst, she was particularly suited for the task. The story of Bournville's housing from 1895 to 1995 is an exciting one and I am happy to give her version of it the fullest commendation.

A centenary is an occasion not just to look back, but to prepare for the future. The housing experiment, which represents all that Bournville stands for, goes on. My fellow Trustees and I are determined to seek out all possible ways to further the Trust's housing work in Bournville and beyond in the years that lie ahead.

Professor Gordon. E. Cherry,
Chairman,

Bournville Village Trust.

19th September, 1994.

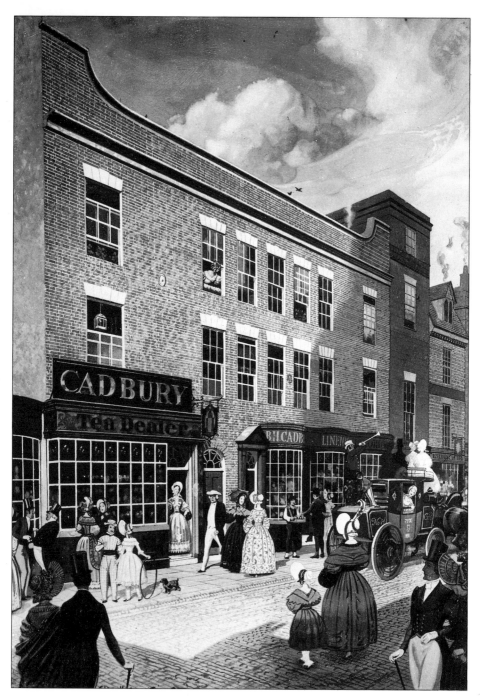

John Cadbury's shop in Bull Street

1. Introduction

Cities have always proved a magnet and springboard for ambition, power and success. But cities also harbour the inadequate, penury, failure and despair.

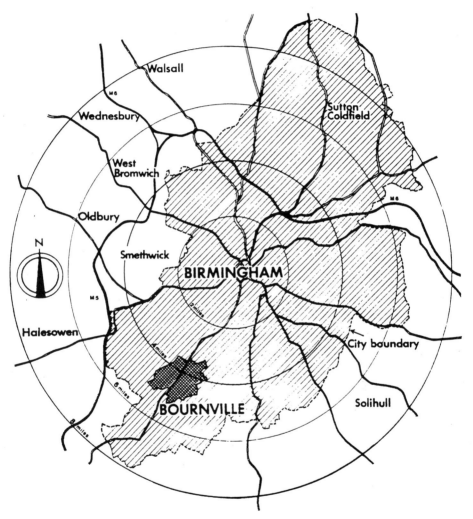

Bournville in relation to the City of Birmingham. The agricultural estates lie outside the City boundaries, to the South

While the ambitious and successful normally look after themselves, the underbelly of the city continues to cause concern. Today it is the turn of the

An engraving of the 'old works' at Bridge Street

inner city – with its dereliction, disused factories, outdated, mainly public, housing and concentrations of people with problems, for which neither they nor society have as yet a solution. Too many young people with too little education, who are often unemployed and too often resort to crime. Too many people who, unlike the ambitious and successful, cannot look after themselves, even for basic living. Too much deliberate vandalism. Drugs too often a common currency.

This grim scenario is normally considered in a totally different context from Bournville Village and the Bournville Village Trust. The Bournville hallmark has, after all, always been associated with garden city development, pleasing houses facing on to wide streets, with plentiful open space and masses of mature trees, a far cry from the hard grey landscape of post-war flats and abandoned factories.

Yet this is the challenge which the Trust has taken on today as it moves outside the boundaries of the garden suburb, into which the village has now grown, and applies 100 years of community development experience and expertise to the existing city scene and an area of urban regeneration. Telford is a new town which successfully rose from industrial dereliction. Birmingham Heartlands, located between the landmark of Spaghetti Junction and the City Centre, was handpicked for regeneration by a special development corporation because of physical blight, poor housing, environment and health, declining education and high levels of unemployment.

It has taken 100 years for the original Bournville Estate of houses for city factory workers in the countryside outside Birmingham to become today's much admired suburb, with its mix of owner-occupiers and tenants, young and old, more and less well off. It will take time, but hopefully not 100 years, to see the impact of its quality of community development elsewhere.

It was, after all, the squalor of the Victorian inner city which inspired the Cadburys to use their personal rewards from running a highly successful business to create a totally new village style of living for people working in the city.

2. BOURNVILLE'S BEGINNINGS

George Cadbury and the Chocolate Business

For George and Richard Cadbury, brought up in a Quaker household in Edgbaston, the city of Birmingham of some 130 years ago presented an opportunity for hard work and achievement in the development of a new industry. Their success provided scope for good industrial practice and philanthropy against the urban backcloth of overcrowding, bad nutrition, ill health and drunken misery, all too prevalent in the fast-developing, smoke-ridden industrial centres of the day.

The two Cadbury brothers took over their father's small business in 1861. Selling tea, coffee, mustard and, amongst other things, 'cocoa nibs', described as a nutritious beverage for breakfast, he had set up a grocer's shop 37 years earlier. Chocolate for eating did not become available until the 1860s and the drinking brew, pounded out by hand with pestle and mortar, was, by modern standards, a strange hybrid mixture including potato starch, sago flour and treacle. The business nevertheless expanded and held a Royal warrant by the time Richard and George succeeded their father at the ages of 25 and 21 .

At work by 7am, George would return to leafy Edgbaston for lunch and work until 9pm except in summer when the day's work started even earlier to allow time off for recreation. At weekends, he helped with the adult school movement teaching young men to read and write.

The business did not prove an immediate runaway success. Indeed the two brothers, like many smaller companies today, nearly closed down when they believed there was a danger that they would begin to run into debt. Richard had decided he would become a surveyor, George had plans for emigration to India as a tea planter. Luckily, however, their economic fortunes turned and in 1866 the brothers introduced a new process from the Netherlands for making pure cocoa. From this point, there was no holding back. They were able to move on to manufacture chocolate bars and fancy filled chocolates, which, nestling in opulent boxes adorned with pictorial designs by Richard, successfully undermined previous French domination of the market.

By 1878, with 2,000 employees, their city centre premises were too small and the two brothers bought 15 acres in the countryside, little more than four miles from the centre, but with good railway and canal access, a trout stream and a cottage called Bournbrook. With due deference to their French rivals and a hint of the urban visionary to come, Bournbrook became, not Bourn Works or Bourn Town but Bournville, a town in waiting.

A view of Bournville looking north from Bournville Lane before development. Early 1880's. Stocks Wood is in the distance

Seeds of Garden Cities

The chocolate manufactory went from strength to strength in production and industrial practice. Cadbury was the first firm to abandon the six-day working week for one of five and a half days and soon provided sports fields, education and outings. Special arrangements were made to reduce the cost of transport from the inner city and a small number of houses built for essential workers.

However, to run a good business and treat their staff as members of the working family did not satisfy the overwhelming social concern of George Cadbury, in particular, about the way so many people were forced to live.
It is difficult today to appreciate the awfulness of city life with which the

Cadburys had come into daily contact and which they had effectively left behind. Most people in Britain now have a roof over their heads, eat regular meals, afford clothes (even if they are second-hand), watch television and video, potter about in gardens, seek financial support from the state if in need and turn to national health services when they are ill. They also live on average for more than 70 years.

Yew Tree Farm Estate before development

But life in Victorian Birmingham was very different. As Joseph Chamberlain, the city's great civic leader and national politician, once told the council: 'We bring up a population in the dark, dreary filthy alleys such as are to be found throughout the area: we surround them with noxious influences of every kind and place them under conditions in which the observance of even ordinary decency is impossible. And what is the result? What can we expect from this sort of thing? The fact is it is no more the fault of these people that they are vicious and intemperate than it is their fault that they are stunted, deformed, debilitated and diseased.'

Houses were crammed together and ill ventilated. Coal smoke particles polluted the air. Unbalanced diets led to rickets and bandy legs. Death often came early. Even at the turn of the century, life expectancy was only about 40 years. Small wonder that some people turned to alcohol for temporary oblivion or that non-conformists believed that same alcohol a source of much social evil. Small wonder too that young men from Britain's cities were pale, puny beings, unfit for work, unfit for battle, a fact which became all too apparent in the Boer War, when, an example quoted by George Cadbury at the annual gathering of Bournville tenants, of 10,000 Manchester men who applied to enlist in 1900, only 1,000 were found fit to serve. If their miserable existence won little awareness or compassion in some sections of society, fear for the future of Britain as a strong nation and empire caused many to voice concern.

As intellectuals, philanthropists and politicians discussed the increasingly obvious social side effects of the industrial revolution, the seeds of a very

It was monotonous housing of this kind which acted as a catalyst for George Cadbury's policy of low density housing amongst green open spaces

A classic example of Victorian slums and social neglect, the side effects of the industrial revolution

different lifestyle emerged which focused on visions of ideal villages and utopian towns. Disraeli wrote of an enlightened industrialist in his novel Sybil. Model housing featured in the 1851 Great Exhibition in Hyde Park. The Irish Quaker, John Richardson, built special housing for workers in his linen factory at Bessbrook. In Yorkshire, the Saltaire village was created for the good of the workers – and of course the mill. Mr. W.H. Lever (later Lord Leverhulme) moved his factory outside Liverpool and developed 32 acres into well laid-out landscaped housing, again for his workers, at Port Sunlight. One Ebenezer Howard, a shorthand writer who had emigrated to and returned from the United States, began shaping ideas for a garden city in debate with contemporaries.

"We bring up a population in dark dreary filthy alleys" Joseph Chamberlain

Long caught up in this foment of opinion and practical experiment, George Cadbury decided to translate ideas into action and see whether it was feasible to build decent homes, not just for his workers but for people at large. In 1893, he bought 120 acres to prevent the disappearance of local countryside under the spreading tentacles of the growing city. The following year, he quietly looked for someone to manage the project and wrote to Mr. A.P. Walker of Cockermouth asking for details of his experience and availability and whether

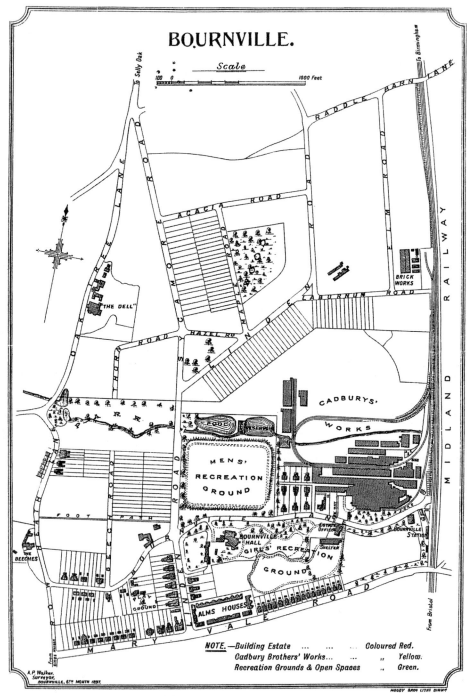

BOURNVILLE.

Scale

1000 Feet

Map of the Estate. A. P. Walker June 1897.

10

or not he was a Quaker. George Cadbury, who stressed that his name should not yet be mentioned in connection with the scheme, said he did not care for anyone who did not enter into the spirit of the undertaking as a labour for the Lord. 'So far as I can ascertain,' he went on, 'there is nothing of the kind in England yet carried out on the principles that I should like to adopt.'

Mr. Walker took the job and the Bournville Estate went on site in 1895. Aimed at respectable citizens on normal wages, the new houses and cottages were relatively simple in design but unusual in that they were substantially endowed with land.

The interior of a typical slum dwelling

The concept to provide the equivalent of village life for the urban working classes, was indeed revolutionary and provided a practical demonstration of the kind of ideas which Ebenezer Howard was to publish three years later in his first version of a work which later became known as Garden Cities of Tomorrow. In 1899, the Cadburys, Mr. Lever and the Rowntrees supported the creation of the new Garden City Association and in 1901 its first conference was held at Bournville, already a sizeable garden village and a garden town in the making. At the end of the previous year, the Estate had been transferred complete with endowment of land to the new Bournville Village Trust to ensure continuity of the vision including necessary development controls.

From that point, the garden city movement gathered strength. The Rowntrees launched New Earswick, a new village outside York, in 1902 and the following year it was the turn of Letchworth, under the banner of First Garden City Ltd., a private limited dividend company led by Ebenezer Howard. Hampstead Garden Suburb went on site a few years later.

Also in the early years of the century, George Cadbury was amongst opinion formers who lobbied for the first town planning act, writing to the responsible MP that, if there were thousands of Bournvilles, which there would be if a bill was passed, his own little experiment would be lost in the crowd.

In 1916, Lloyd George, then Minister for Munitions of War, thanked him for help in the erection of temporary housing for local munitions workers. George Cadbury replied that one great object of his life had been to improve the housing conditions of the people of this country. 'A child brought up in the back streets of our cities is handicapped in mind, body and spirit,' he wrote adding that children of 12 years of age brought up in Bournville were on average two and a half inches taller with three inch bigger chests than comparable inner city children. He went on: 'I am now in my seventy-seventh year and the strain of public life is over and I can rejoice in the thought of any little service to my fellow man. You have done magnificent service in the past and it may help you to know the earnest desire of many of your fellow citizens that you may be spared with health and strength for further service and at last, when life's journey is over, hear the joyful words – 'Well done, thou good and faithful servant, enter thou into the joy of thy Lord' . Your sincere friend.'

George Cadbury carried on as chairman of the Bournville trust for another six years and lived until his mid-nineties by which time he could begin to see the evolution of his early ideas and idealism. But what was Bournville like as a place?

Early Days on the Estate

When Bournville started off 100 years ago, it was designed as a fair-sized housing estate set in the rolling Midlands countryside. The works, as Midlands factories are still known had been built about 15 years before and the railway provided transport for workers who lived in the city and commuted out of town to the factory in a garden.

But the city was growing rapidly and remorselessly, engulfing green fields and woodlands with seemingly endless terraces of tunnel back housing, the successor to the even more cramped style of development, known as back to back. In such housing, one row of houses literally backed up or was stuck on to the backs of the row behind, the two rows each facing outwards to their respective streets. There was no through ventilation. Tunnel back housing was already a great improvement including extensions, room for a yard and the possibility of through currents of air, so necessary, for any hope of reasonable health.

The first houses to be built on the Bournville Estate Mary Vale Road – started 1895

The Bournville Estate was totally different. The first houses went up at the end of Linden Road, Bournville Lane and Selly Oak Road. Instead of terraces, the new brick houses were built in pairs or groups of four and laid out with gardens, fairly narrow at the front and capacious at the back, where the ground was ready tilled to give the new occupier a good start and lines of fruit trees planted either side of the boundary hedge.

Further development on the Estate this well built home was spacious enough to be converted into a temporary Post Office

One of the first houses to be built on Linden Road 1905

The architecture was straightforward, homely and solid. Appointed Bournville architect in 1895, Alexander Harvey looked to local Worcestershire and Warwickshire villages for his inspiration and followed the local vernacular tradition of brick. There were three bedrooms upstairs and living rooms, kitchen, scullery and bathroom downstairs. In some cases, the bath was sunk in the floor or concealed vertically in a cupboard when out of use. Harvey avoided excessive decoration in his search for economy and harmony, a necessary key to beauty, and only included inglenook fireplaces in the more expensive properties. Jerry building this development most certainly was not. This housing was built to last with the minimum of repairs.

The houses were not cheap and indeed cost more than speculative terraced rivals in nearby burgeoning communities. They offered however a totally different quality of life with gardens front and back, wide tree-lined streets and neighbours kept at reasonable distance. Numbering 143 in all, the homes were sold at cost price on 999-year leases, the leases and small ground rent being imposed to ensure long-term control and continuity of the area's rural appearance. A cottage cost a minimum of £150 and the working man, who could afford a deposit of 50 per cent or more, could qualify for an advance or loan from Mr. Cadbury at 2.5 per cent. If such savings were not available and the deposit was less, then interest charges of three per cent were imposed.

Houses built in 1902. A good example of the housing and planning which made Bournville so distinctive

Harvey's economic use of space in his planning meant that baths could be stored vertically

George Cadbury, unlike most lending institutions, simply wanted the scheme to be self-financing. With £30 down and an annual repayment of £10 plus yearly but reducing interest charges, total payments over 12 years worked out at £173, or £13 16s less than a rent of 6s per week, over the same period of time. It was a good deal. In fact, it was too good a deal. Before long, a number of the early Bournville residents discovered they could realise a profit on the original price and sold off their new homes. This personal gain, however pleasing to the former owner, meant that the prices would all too quickly rise beyond the means of many of the people George Cadbury wanted to help.

So instead of 999-year leases, the next tract of houses were built for rent – the majority at between 6s and 8s 6d a week, a level possible for the hard-working artisan. As direct landlord, George Cadbury could control housing costs and make certain that the profit of good living remained with residents, already present or those to come. Again the rents were not cheap. But he was not trying to solve every problem of urban poverty but to demonstrate the feasibility of building a different type of community in which hard-working people in the city could live healthier, more responsible lives.

The interior of a cottage in 1906. Note the inglenook fireplace

From the very start the green and pleasant landscape was a dominating factor

Unlike Saltaire and Port Sunlight, the Bournville Estate was never tied to the works, although George Cadbury did briefly consider the possibility of creating a Quaker community. By the time building started, however, the development was open to anyone who was attracted to the very different lifestyle of what later became known as *rus in urbe* or the garden city or town.

Green Ethos

From the very start, the green and pleasant landscape was a dominating factor in Bournville. Individual builders were brought in but no one builder was allowed to build more than four houses and the size and style of houses in proportion to site was carefully regulated. No manufactory was permitted or business of any kind, excepting a few convenience shops.

Seven acres were immediately provided for a recreation ground and two or three small plots for children's playgrounds. As proprietor, George Cadbury also promised to give further land for schools, baths and an institute.

Semi-detached or groups of four, the houses or cottages were set back from 42 foot wide tree-lined roads with gardens front and back. Each house occupied but one quarter of its plot and an early prospectus stated that the objective was to make it easy for working men to own houses with large gardens and remain secure in the knowledge that their homes could not be spoilt either by the building of factories or by interference with their enjoyment of sun, light and air.

Fruit trees were planted at the far end of the garden and tenants were expected to grow vegetables to offset the ground rent or rent by as much as 2s a week – and of course benefit from fresh air, exercise and fresh food. Indeed there was nothing to stop the new village settler from keeping bees, chickens or rabbits, but not pigs. In due course, tools could be borrowed and gardeners were available to give advice to new residents, who might well have no previous experience of green living things. Allotments were available for people living in nearby communities and gardening classes held for 'youths'. Indeed gardening was even seen as a helpful and profitable contribution to the problems of part-time work.

Portrait of the Youths gardening class

19

George promised to give land for the recreation of the children on his Estate

Controlling the Future

George Cadbury wanted to make a small contribution to the problem of housing in industrial cities and to show that decent living conditions were economically possible including a small return. However, speculation by some original purchasers and the threat of more profitable, cheaper, higher density housing in the immediately surrounding area forced him to think more deeply about ways to develop, manage and sustain the new community. The long lease already enabled the maintenance of standards of design and landscape and prevented infilling of gardens with additional development where homes had been sold. With the rented housing, high standards could also be maintained. But the enterprise needed to be on a firmer long-term footing if it was to survive without erosion of its overwhelmingly green ethos in the face of normal urban development pressures.

While a limited company would have been possible, George Cadbury chose the mechanism of a trust because it allowed him to lay down lasting objectives, whereas with a company policy would have been subject to the will of shareholders. The terms were carefully laid down. The legal language of the original trust deed is flowery but the intention and details are perfectly clear.

'Whereas the founder is desirous of alleviating the evils which arise from the insanitary and insufficient accommodation supplied to large numbers of the working classes and of securing to workers in factories some of the advantages of outdoor village life with opportunities for the natural and healthful occupation of cultivating the soil,' the deed begins.

The main object, according to the document, concerns: 'the amelioration of the condition of the working class and labouring population in and around Birmingham and elsewhere in Great Britain by the provision of improved dwellings, with gardens and open space, to be enjoyed therewith and by giving them facilities, should the trustees think it desirable to do so, for producing or acquiring the necessaries of life.'

The trustees, originally members of the Cadbury family and now including representatives from Birmingham City Council, Birmingham University and the Society of Friends, were effectively given a free hand in terms of location and means. They were however to continue in the Bournville style. As far as possible, housing was to occupy only a quarter of each site. Rents, if practicable, should be accessible to labouring people from the city while not

A group portrait of the Trustees in 1927 and in 1951

making them recipients of bounty. At least one-tenth of the land was to be devoted to parks and recreation over and above the area taken up by private gardens and roads. Shops and factories were to occupy no more than one-fifteenth of the land. No public house or building for the manufacture, sale or distribution of intoxicating liquor should be allowed without the unanimous consent of trustees in writing and any subsequent profits were to be spent on alternative recreation. There was to be no sectarian or political bias.

With some 313 houses and 330 acres – a considerable endowment then worth £172,000 – George Cadbury launched the trust on December 14, 1900. At first, he presided over weekly meetings which would discuss the building programme, mix, development of the community, in particular, a village council, means of encouraging gardening, including competitions, and ways of promoting knowledge of the experiment through lectures, publications and organised visits. There were further endowments including shares in Letchworth and Hampstead Garden Suburb, not to mention a number of public buildings for the village including the church and school. 'I have seriously considered how far a man is justified in giving away the heritage of his children and have come to the conclusion that my children will be all the better off for being deprived of this money, ' he told an American interviewer in 1902.

3. A SERIES OF INITIATIVES

Robin Hood Principle

Bournville has always aimed to remain in the vanguard and encouraged initiatives in housing design, purpose and management ranging from, in the early days, housing for the elderly and the single professional woman, when few women had jobs, to self build, equity sharing and the use of solar energy. This desire to tackle new problems, without compromise to overall standards, has undoubtedly injected vitality into a community which could all too easily have simply developed into a mixture of well landscaped social housing and larger up-market owner-occupied areas in a succession of shady tree-lined avenues, crescents and culs-de-sac.

BOURNVILLE BIRMINGHAM · RESIDENTIAL CLUB FOR WOMEN · ARCHITECT S. ALEX WILMOT ESTATE OFFICE BOURNVILLE

Although George Cadbury provided the main driving force at Bournville, his older brother Richard also played an active role, in particular conceiving a Robin Hood approach for providing housing and services to older people. In today's jargon, his method might perhaps best be described as planning gain. Instead of robbing the rich to give to the poor, Richard Cadbury let 35 larger houses to create an endowment fund for the separate trust responsible for building and maintaining the nearby quadrangle of 33 alms houses he also erected in 1897.

The trust also provided necessary medicine and medical services. This principle – disposing of property to create funds for social projects – has proved useful at Bournville on more than one occasion, most recently in 1992 when a former Cadbury property was bought by the trust and, after new leases were negotiated, sold for about £1,500,000 profit. This sum has since been invested in an endowment or social fund to use on a roll-forward basis. As a start, a small amount is to help tenants to afford high levels of rent on property bought as a new venture by Bournville in the inner city.

The almshouses which Richard Cadbury built in 1897 on Mary Vale Road

Over the years, the elderly have continued as an area of special need in Bournville with the provision of bungalows, sheltered accommodation and homes with partial nursing facilities for the very frail. Projects frequently involve other specialist organisations. For example, Midlands Electricity plc, Birmingham University's Centre of Applied Gerontology and the Trust combined forces to equip a house with additional facilities for the elderly. Elsewhere separate homes have been staffed for individuals with different forms of mental handicap or learning difficulties so that they can stay within the community. In such cases, Bournville acts as a catalyst for outside interests, identifying suitable property, helping to raise capital funds and running costs and then taking over as managing agents.

Role for Housing Societies

The ability to help housing societies has provided a means for Bournville to widen the scope and type of people for which it caters and, at the same time, encouraged individuals to take more responsibility for solving their own problems. Following an earlier example in Ealing, London, Bournville Tenants Ltd. was set up as a cooperative venture in 1906. The society agreed to lease 20 acres for 99 years and build between 144 and 198 houses (145 were eventually built). Two acres were provided rent free to ensure sufficient open space and George Cadbury gave the society a village hall, trees for the roads, fruit trees for the gardens and creepers and flowers to grow at the front. Basically all the members bought shares for £1 each, arranged for Bournville's architect to design the houses and a committee of management was set up to set the rent and rules. By 1911, there were 261 members with between three and 200 shares apiece, who had subscribed £8,850 on their own account and, as a result, been able to borrow £20,680. A number of houses have since been sold under the right-to-buy legislation but the society still has its own committee of management with the trust acting as managing agents.

In 1919 Bournville Works set up a similar housing society for people employed at the chocolate factory and built about 360 homes.

Bournville Village Trust was originally established to concentrate on the needs of the labouring working classes but, by the beginning of the first world war, there were signs of the emergence of a different working class in offices and the service sector including clerks and shop assistants. Their aspirations and means were slightly higher and another type of housing society, called Weoley Hill Limited, was created to provide suitable homes for sale on 99-year leases. Because of the war, little progress was made until 1921 when a local builder leased the land, used the Trust's architect and built and sold the houses. At this point the society was dissolved. The Woodlands Housing Society was a similar venture.

Whilst the Bournville Village Trust was achieving great advancement in housing provision, by the late 20's–30's housing in the City had little changed since the previous Century

Self-Build in Quantity

Self-build appeals in theory to many people's instinctive wish to construct from scratch their ideal home. For the most part, satisfaction of this desire comes from do-it-yourself using flat packs to create fitted kitchens. There will nevertheless always be small groups of people who are prepared to forgo other leisure pursuits and, with some guidance, invest sweat and equity in building the whole house.

After the second world war, Bournville was well equipped with land to help a number of such groups to achieve this end. Most of the original self-builders were former service men with little hope of council houses or flats, who joined together with colleagues at work and brought in a number of skilled tradesmen to help. Some groups were quite large with up to 48 members. Because of shortages and the need for building licences, the first four had to take the form of co-partnerships, which meant they ended up as tenants, but most individuals were eventually able to own the handiwork which became their homes.

Generally the members would form a society to negotiate terms for the lease of land and house plans on which it raised money from a building society or possibly the Public Works Loans Board. The Trust made financing somewhat easier by undertaking necessary infrastructure works, such as roads and sewers, and including these costs in the ground rent to be paid annually over succeeding years. In due course ownership and mortgages were transferred from the lending body to each individual and the housing society was wound down. Early groups of Cadbury employees and Post Office workers were followed by self-builders from Lucas, Austin, building tradesmen and the fire service.

Although bungalows were built in the very first scheme, two-storey housing became the norm, semi-detached and terraces, with weekend supervision on a voluntary basis by an architect from the Trust offices. The self-builder could save about half the cost so that a house in the mid 1960s cost some £2,000 compared with £4,000 if bought from a builder. As demand grew, the Trust designed first a group of about 70 houses, which were taken up by six self-build societies, and then an area of almost twice as many homes to be built again by several groups. In all, more than 400 homes, or about five per cent of Bournville, were and are self-build.

Sunshine Houses

Bournville's first experiment in the realm of what is now called solar energy was launched in the 1930s recession. The principle was simple, sensible and against current social practice. At that time, and often nowadays, the living room with its bigger windows was automatically placed regardless of aspect at the front, the kitchen at the back. With the sunshine houses, if the south and therefore the sun was at the back, then the room format was swung round to benefit from the extra light and warmth and so save on bills. The kitchen looked north over the public realm.

In the late 1970's, as an experiment in energy saving and cost control, a solar hot water system was installed in a block of sheltered flats for the elderly with collectors angled into the roof under patent glazing. This was followed by a second scheme – also flats for older people and involving computerised control and two banks of plastic collectors in the roof, this time facing south east and south west to increase their potential for heat absorption.

The breakthrough came with the design of Bournville's solar village in which maximum sunshine and energy conservation principles were applied over a

10 Shilling Houses or Sunshine Homes Griffins Brook Lane

wider area of development and to different types of house. The opportunity arose with the sale of Rowheath by Bournville Works to the city and the subsequent 99-year lease of the land to the Trust – about 20 acres for development and about twice this area for retention as open space including playing fields. With the help of locally based consultants and funding from the European Community, the scheme provided bungalows for the elderly, sheltered accommodation, family homes and gardens and a demonstration house. A number of firms of architects were involved as well as those working with the Trust.

Rowheath – sheltered accommodation on the Estate. This was an experiment in the use of solar energy

The sheltered housing is planned around two courtyards with all flats facing south and sufficient space to allow low-angle winter sun into the ground floor. Corridors are located on the north side of the buildings and communal rooms on the east-west axis. The walls are coated to absorb and retain more radiation and sliding shutters cover windows at night which, when moved into place in front of the windows, allow retained heat into the rooms. A second scheme for the elderly includes a power generator designed to operate on solar energy.

Family houses were designed more simply but with large windows for solar gain facing within at least 20° off south, while windows facing north are small and all are double glazed. They also include thermal blinds mainly for use at night to prevent heat loss. Insulation is higher than normal and special internal concrete blocks store and release heat gained during the day. The demonstration house was designed as a testbed with added features including buffer spaces, solar heated hot water supplies, photovoltaic solar cells and computer controls capable of powering lights and television for a limited number of hours per day. Regular monitoring of this and five other houses showed that solar energy provided 34 per cent of heat in the family house.

Subsequently a wider survey indicated that 95 per cent homes had lower energy bills than in their former properties and almost as many occupants believed their heating bills were below average. Energy has continued as a topic for practical study with, in 1993, a study comparing the use of gas and electricity for heating new bungalows.

Christopher Taylor Court. A sheltered scheme for the elderly

These houses built around green open space have energy saving features standard such as solar blinds, wall to ceiling insulation and double glazing. Part of the solar village

Equity Share or Part Ownership

One area of the solar energy village was also used to provide an opportunity for equity sharing to help first-time buyers gain a foothold on the housing ladder and local people, who were renting property elsewhere in Bournville, were given priority. More than a third of the properties were taken up by former tenants who decided they would like and could afford to buy one quarter and rent the other three-quarters in the hope, over time, of increasing their ownership share. Because of the housing market collapse at the end of the 1980s, few have as yet been able to climb onto the next sharing step.

The Trust had already applied the principle of equity sharing in 1983 to the Laurence Court development of 22 flats for older people. For that scheme a special housing association had to be created to allow the sale of a 70 per cent share to individuals or couples, who then rented the other 30 per cent and paid their share of management overheads. When owners or tenants leave or die, 70 per cent of the updated value is returned.

An elderly couple enjoy the benefits of their flat at Laurence Court

Laurence Court, a sheltered Housing Scheme of 22 flats for the elderly

4. CHANGING PRESSURES

Bournville People

Because of the role taken by a number of industrial leaders and philanthropists in providing housing for their working men, it is widely believed that Bournville is, or at least was originally, another tied estate or village. As such, it might be of interest as a development focused on workers at the local factory, which presumably brought the company due reward in kind as health, strength, morale and happiness improved. It would also be interesting in view of its size and style.

However, while the Cadburys were undoubtedly successful businessmen, who expanded their market by concentrating on quality, the village development for George Cadbury was a pragmatic attempt in tackling the inner city evils of bad housing, dirt, overcrowding, ill health and alcoholism. He wanted to show that good living conditions were within the grasp of the ordinary, respectable, hard-working man. Within this category Bournville catered for all-comers. Workers at the factory were made welcome but they never formed more than 40 per cent of the total. Today the Trust remains circumspect about detailed analysis, for example of census figures or special surveys, designed to pinpoint exactly how many individuals live in Bournville, of what age, with what job (if any). With its paternalistic origins and despite a strong desire to remain at the leading edge of housing provision, the trust wants Bournville's people to feel comfortable, not endlessly observed as some sociological zoo.

In 1900 there were 313 homes, in 1939, 2,197 of which 815 were let and 1,382 sold on long lease. Today there are some 7,600 properties in Bournville and perhaps some 20,000 people. About 3,750 residents are owner-occupiers, the majority on long lease including the self-build homes. Just under 3,900 householders are tenants, of whom some 60 per cent rent their houses and flats directly from the trust. The rest include a mixture of housing associations, local authority and special tenancies. In 1901, 51 per cent tenants were factory workers and 13 per cent clerks and similar occupations.

Welcoming the Homeless

Even if today there is no similar recent breakdown, changes have occurred in society during the intervening years, which have affected the social make-up and therefore the community at large. The labourer of the late nineteenth century who could afford to rent a Bournville home, if he spent enough time in his garden nurturing fruit and vegetables, no longer plays the same crucial function. As the city of 1,000 trades, Birmingham then was a manufacturing city in which people undertook most of the production. Today in Britain's second city, and indeed the country at large, the manufacturing sector has shrunk, automated processes have in large measure replaced men and women on the shop floor and services have become major employers. Birmingham city centre has meanwhile been transformed into a hub for business conventions, the arts, shopping, the professions and a host of often unseen back-up jobs.

Once established, today's new solid respectable service worker probably buys his or her own home. In the meantime they are unlikely to find a place to rent in Bournville. Nowadays, as Bournville homes fall vacant, they are offered to people in need, either from the city's waiting list or that of the Trust. Both are broadly similar in their definition of need except that the Trust refuses to raise false hope and therefore excludes people unless it believes a home can be found within approximately one year.

The Trust has long since lost total independence over the allocation of its rented properties, let alone those on long lease, which are sold on the open market. As a result, it cannot really influence the overall social mix of its population. There is a £1,000,000 annual programme for major refurbishment, rents can fund little new investment and there is no more land to sell. However, as a registered housing association, the Trust has been able to turn to the Housing Corporation, although the percentage of such government funds towards development costs has been gradually squeezed over recent years as private finance has been encouraged to lend on the basis of likely rents. As a quid pro quo for financial help, housing associations are required to accept a proportion of nominations from the local housing list and, in 1994, the Trust agreed to offer the city 50 per cent of all vacancies, in addition to those financed by public funding, in return for an opportunity for the trust to develop elsewhere in Birmingham on city-owned land. In Bournville itself, the Trust has also bought land from the city and had therefore to accept the city's choice of tenants.

While undoubtedly this arrangement helps those in housing need – in 1993, 58 per cent of lettings went to the homeless, 17 per cent to single parent families – many of the people who move into Bournville these days are no longer self supporting and generally less able to cope. They may have no job or training or indeed any skills and, while housing and other benefits can provide for immediate needs, they also create a poverty trap from which only the exceptional individual can escape. The Trust receives due rent but is faced by a growing proportion of people who may have little knowledge of or respect for Bournville traditions. Graffiti can be and is removed as quickly as possible but, for the area to retain its special nature, newcomers have to accept responsibilities as well as rights. And while the Trust cannot hope to solve all the problems of society, Bournville has to find ways to absorb the growing numbers of these new individuals and families without allowing the quality of life in any area to deteriorate.

Their very arrival can, according to James Wilson, the Trust's Chief Executive, have for them an uplifting effect. 'We cannot do anything about the poverty of people who are arriving. But we can encourage them to look after gardens and houses in such a way that they're taking pride in the environment in which they live and this has a ripple invisible effect on the way they behave and the way they bring up their children.' He is also hopeful that the very fact that Bournville, unlike the inner city from which they come, is a community composed of people in very different income brackets means that newcomers have a chance to meet a cross-section of society from which ideas, behaviour and opportunities can perhaps rub off.

The Green, the centre of the old village looking the same as it did in George Cadbury's day

Maintaining a Green Scene

It is perhaps through its landscape that Bournville excels. The area displays a lushness, a vision of mature trees, green space and parkland all too rare in British cities, yet comparable, oddly as it may seem, to suburbs in North America. Across the Atlantic, building lots have frequently been spacious and it is common practice – as in Bournville – for front gardens to flow into pavements and the street without the stone or brick walls, fences and hedges, with which the British so often defend their personal castles behind rose beds and front lawns.

All too little research has been undertaken into the psychological benefits of parks and open space, let alone this form of community open plan. But the combination of tree-lined street and green, often flowering frontages creates an enjoyable sense of community wealth and laid-back wellbeing. It makes so many places, including much new development, feel mean and cramped. While instinct proclaims the advantages of space and greenery for the spirit or soul, the spin-off for inhabitants remains unproven – except of course that Bournville homes do sell at a premium.

A keen gardener on the estate demonstrates that the cultivation of home grown produce is not dead

Bournville is of course blessed by the underlying rolling nature of the land and the organic planning of the area, to meet new needs, made full use of stream beds and steep inclines to enhance the network of open space and foot paths. The ability of long leaseholders to buy the freehold of their homes under the 1967 Act obviously affected existing shared arrangements for maintaining the landscape. Within five years, however, the Trust won High Court approval for a management scheme to ensure continued high standards of design and landscape and with power to fix a management charge of £3 rising every five

Two young residents living on the Trust's most recent housing development will inherit an environment which has retained all the features and benefits of a green and well maintained landscape.

years. The scheme also included arrangements for a special estate management committee consisting of four trustees and four residents elected from the four different areas of Bournville.

Landscape is of course alive and constantly but slowly changes, as do human beings throughout their lives. Apart from normal maintenance, the Trust has to bear in mind the developing shape and appearance so that, for example, new trees have time to grow to retain today's present image as older specimens need replacing. In the 1980s, landscape consultants were appointed to survey and produce a master plan for Bournville, which pointed to the need to mow 345,000 square metres grass, regularly trim 21.6 kilometres of hedgerows, maintain 11,000 shrubs, thin out and generally look after 38100 sq. m. woodlands and prune 25,200 sq.m. rose beds. While the balanced programme to ensure the area's continuing pleasing appearance requires, as might be expected, greater regular investment, the report also highlighted what many saw as an unfair division of costs between Bournville tenants and Bournville owners, whether freehold or long leasehold.

Obviously every resident benefits from the green scene. However, rent from tenants was contributing disproportionately to this necessary expenditure because the charges fixed by the High Court for long leaseholders no longer covered their proper share of actual costs, even though such property owners gain financially in the future, as well as in their everyday lives, when they come to sell. In 1991 the trust went back to the High Court and the system was made more tenable.

Upkeep of front and back gardens is a different matter and some Bournville tenants these days find little joy in developing any talent for green fingers. Some may also have too little cash or time. Implements and plants cost money and the size of some gardens can well be daunting to a young mother with children or couple whose knowledge is limited to cut flowers in vases and vegetables sold ready scrubbed in see-through plastic in the supermarket.

In the early years of the century, the Trust arranged courses in gardening and loaned out tools backed up by advice. At the end of the twentieth century, the welter of produce available from all the earth's corners and state income support, combined with television at home and outside leisure attractions a-plenty, can turn gardening into a burden. Yet Bournville gardens are part of its ethos and culture.

The Trust has reintroduced competitions for the best kept front garden but new ways have to be found to cultivate a gardening community among new tenants so that they can perhaps turn to neighbours, their tenants association, community council or the Trust for help. The contribution of such smallholdings may be one means to provide people with too little paid work with a reasonable occupation and fresh food. In fact, with the right promotion and back-up, the wheel could perhaps turn full circle to renew George Cadbury's emphasis on the advantages of gardens as a source of health and some wealth.

Permission for Change

Bournville's architecture is quiet. Brick houses, mainly two storeys high, some flats, are set back from roads singly in pairs and small blocks, well framed by the landscaped street scene, in some areas 100 years old. Closer inspection reveals differences, evolutionary rather than revolutionary, in the manner of the traditional English village, where time and respect for context blur the sometimes harsh edges of change. The excitement and often unsettling nature of post-war modernism have been ignored in favour of an updated Midlands idiom, existing ideas constantly fine tuned to suit each decade. Experiments with other materials have been brief and the well liked Warwickshire/Worcestershire style has prevailed.

The same is true of changes and additions, which individuals wish to make as times and ideas change. The trust insists on seeing and approving all proposals before submission to Birmingham City Council for any necessary planning permission. There are two conservation areas in or near the original village centre but in effect the trust operates a conservation philosophy throughout. Sensible and different design guidelines are issued for different areas and all point out that Bournville can only keep its special environment if new development or alterations are considered within the context of the neighbourhood. In the older areas, double glazing is suggested to avoid replacing attractive small paned windows and the trust prevents side extensions creating makeshift terraces by closing the gap between individual properties. The system applies to the removal of chimneys or hedges as well as new construction such as a garage, conservatory or extension or modern impedimenta like burglar alarms, solar panels and satellite dishes.

Managing the Car

The advent of mass car ownership has brought problems to Bournville, as is the case elsewhere. Chunks of front gardens vanish under hardstanding, garages are built and the community must be grateful that there is in many areas the space for this to happen without too great an impact on the environment. But many of the roads were designed when traffic was light and cars now stream through with little regard for people on foot. In addition, the chocolate experience at Cadbury World draws more than 460,000 visitors into the edge of the old village every year. So far there is all too little much-needed traffic calming, whether in the form of sleeping policemen, flat-topped tables or chokes to keep speed down in this primarily residential area. The Trust here finds itself in a quandary in that the roads are public, management measures are expensive and it feels the city ought to pay. On the other hand, an evolving district of such high quality in so many respects including management might expect traffic control to feature in its overall quality of environment.

Involving the Community

The issue is also one for the community and the Trust has, since its very early days, tried to involve residents in discussion of issues relating to their future. The Bournville Village Council was formed in 1902 and other groups have since come into being in the different areas. While the Trust's origins were undoubtedly paternal, its present composition, with members of the Cadbury family and representatives from the City, the University and the Society of Friends, is perhaps not the best means of encouraging greater independence and participation or obviously relevant to its expanding role. And, of course, many people are busy, have long journeys to work and, unless things really go awry, quite happy to let others run the community which they enjoy.

Like gardens and landscape the individual quality of housing in Bournville is updated and improved and the residents maintain their homes to the highest standard

The Trust, however, wants to encourage more direct community involvement. Representatives of residents sit on management committees for housing and the Estate as a whole including applications for changes to property. A trust has been established to run the Rowheath sport and community centre and one area committee has recently taken on responsibility for the management including finances of its local village hall.

As in any new town, the change from development to management of change is difficult, particularly in an area as distinctive as Bournville in a city as large and vital as Birmingham.

5. THE WAY AHEAD

Infill or Passive Contentment?

Like gardens, landscapes, homes and indeed cities, organisations have to be pruned and renewed or wither and, even if they do not die, languish in increasing obscurity with little left of purpose or new achievement. Already homes at Bournville have been updated and improved and this programme will continue as part of the continuing maintenance of an important asset, which is of course home and home town or community for many thousands of people.

So far as the Trust is concerned, each chairman has brought his or her own particular stimulus and enthusiasm to this ongoing multifaceted experiment in urban living. Nevertheless the trust too, under its current chairman, Professor Gordon Cherry, the first not to have a Cadbury family connection, has recently turned the spotlight on the way ahead.

Except for the odd pocket of land, Bournville is now fully developed, a suburb with an individual quality of lifestyle and landscape in Britain's second city. At one time, the trust was prepared to buy in a number of long-lease properties which came on the market with a view to long-term redevelopment. The very action however provoked debate and a decision not to proceed down that particular avenue. Bournville gardens might well be spacious enough for the insertion of backland mews and bungalows or many more homes at much higher density in the rebuilding of an area as a whole. But where then would be the difference, the special place and purpose? Bournville could all too easily become a piece of acceptable but ordinary suburb, overwhelmed by time and relegated to the history of British housing and town planning.

The Trust could also have decided to sit back, content with past success, simply caring for Bournville more or less as it is today – renting vacant property, undertaking sensible refurbishment, supervising minor change, planting replacement trees, generally maintaining the landscape and encouraging the residents to take over the running, where possible, of community affairs. After all, the Dickensian conditions of the mid to late Victorian era have long since vanished and government has largely picked up the challenge of the early campaigning intellectuals and industrial philanthropists, who proved, by their deeds, that good housing, combined with clean air, sunlight and a better diet, very quickly improved the length and quality of life for those who formerly lived in big city slums.

Bournville Diversities

Instead of resting on its laurels, the Trust has however decided to look beyond the territory directly associated with the Bournville hallmark and stamp its ethos of quality community development – not social ghettos – elsewhere. The trust's original terms, carefully drawn for flexibility and expansion, have provided the necessary framework: 'the amelioration of the condition of the working class and labouring population in and around Birmingham and elsewhere in Great Britain by the provision of improved dwellings with gardens and open space to enjoy therewith.'

Bournville today, as was the case 100 years ago, may not be able to tackle all problems associated with poverty including training and employment. But it has design, development and management expertise which can perhaps work in other situations.

In the early 1980s, the Trust became involved in a joint project with Birmingham City and a building society for a housing action area. The city planned to undertake block or envelope improvements to the outside of buildings with the trust helping owners upgrade their properties from within. More recently the Trust has become a partner in Telford, the former new town, where it plans to apply the Bournville philosophy and practice to an existing environment. By the end of 1993, the Trust had built up a holding of 360 homes, mostly rented, a few on shared equity. A number of flats for single people have since been built.

As well as the Shropshire town, Bournville has also decided to see how best it can help improve life in the inner city of Birmingham itself. As a development corporation which originated from the enterprise of Birmingham City Council and the local business community, Heartlands has a distinctive approach in its remit to transform deprived and derelict lands hardly one mile from the city centre. Here Wimpey is building and the Trust is acquiring and will manage a small slice of city or new community – 29 flats for rent, four shops, a dental surgery and a new community centre.

2000 and Beyond

In 1993 the Trust approved a new statement of purpose, mission and business plan to take its work forward to the year 2000 and beyond. As was the case with George Cadbury in 1895, the Trust still aims to build and manage communities, not simply homes. In undertaking this role, it operates in a different league from most housing associations, a number of which may own and manage larger numbers of homes but have no community development remit.

The Trust's aims include: the promotion of quality houses and flats for a mix of people, although concentrating on those with insufficient means to help themselves; the best possible estate and housing management with the encouragement of residents, if they so wish, to share in decisions which affect them; the promotion of ways to improve the quality of community life; the promotion of developments with distinctive architecture and landscape and opportunities for shops, recreation and community activities.

By 2000 and the year of the trust's centenary, as well as having some 4,000 rented homes to manage, it would dearly like to start building a second Bournville or New Bournville, an urban village which could perhaps take on board current thinking about sustainability in both the individual home and the community, capitalise on its experience with solar energy and conservation and perhaps create pedestrian oases linked by footpaths, cycle ways and public transport with cars left on the edge as in some holiday villages.

Theoretically Bournville has the land – some 3,000 acres farm and woodland on the edge of Birmingham. However these acres lie in the green belt and were bought specifically to preserve countryside on the city's edge. In addition, the case for recycling dead lands within existing towns and cities is strong. And unless conceived as a teleworking and dormitory town, a second Bournville also needs an economic raison d'etre – the twentieth century equivalent of a chocolate works – not necessarily just to provide local jobs for local residents but to instill the vitality, hard edge, purpose and perhaps new philanthropy which distinguishes Birmingham and other Midlands cities from, for example, fading genteel retirement resorts.

In the 100 years since the first families moved into the Bournville Estate, the country has endured two world wars, watched the European Union develop and enjoyed massive social and economic improvement. Bournville itself, a green town now embraced by Birmingham, has during this period played both local and national roles. Human nature is such that for the visionaries of each generation there must be new problems to solve, new holy grails on the horizon. If someone with the same energy, social awareness and missionary zeal as George Cadbury were to expand his or her business from central Birmingham today, he or she might, given most people's generally good health, now wish to concentrate on other problems as well as housing and help people in the inner city learn new skills, find and create jobs, become more financially independent and fight crime.

In moving into Telford and Heartlands, the Bournville Village Trust is flexing its muscles in exciting, untried territory, which should lead to new ideas, for example for training and jobs, as well as the chance to adapt the Bournville style of housing and community development to existing towns and the inner city. As a quality hallmark, Bournville is hard to beat. The Trust now has the challenge of imposing that hallmark on areas which need every ounce of quality they can absorb and imaginative initiatives as novel as the garden city was 100 years ago.